The Noah and Logan Children's Book Series

Volume One - Stories one to five.

By

Benjamin K. M. Kellogg

To the Egans,

I hope You enjoy these stories.

Happy Reading!

Benjamin K. M. Kellogg

The Noah and Logan Children's Book Series

Volume One - Stories one to five.

By

Benjamin K. M. Kellogg

© 2018

Published by Ex-L-Ence Publishing, a division of Winghigh Limited, England.

ISBN: 978-1-909133-99-0

Contents

About The Author

Born in 1991, Benjamin is an autistic adult and a life-long resident of a small village in central New York State, USA. He graduated summa cum laude from Cayuga Community College in 2012 with an Associate Degree in Arts in Humanities and Social Science with a concentration in writing.

Since his graduation, he has been pursuing a career in freelance writing. He also maintains a personal blog, www.kellogthoughts.com, where he shares his thoughts and perspectives about movies, television, books, videogames, professional wrestling (especially WWE), and anything else on his mind.

Benjamin created the "Noah and Logan" children's book series as a way to help children with autism learn the social and life skills he struggled with as a child. He sincerely hopes his written works are of help to and enjoyed by readers everywhere.

The illustrations for Ben's books are done by his mum, Theresa, based on Ben's ideas.

Dedication

To Noah and Logan with love.

Story One

Noah and Logan Learn to Clean

Welcome to Noah and Logan's playroom!

Noah and Logan are having fun.

Look at all the toys on the floor. There is a **green** top and a **yellow** truck and a **brown** teddy bear and an **orange** and **purple** ball.

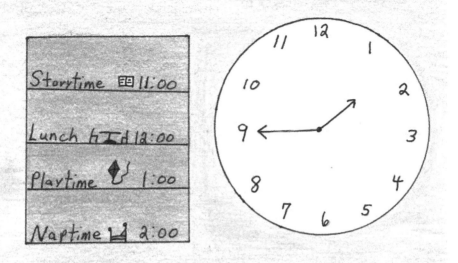

It is almost nap time.

Time to clean up the playroom!

Logan picks up the **green** top and the **orange** and **purple** ball. He places the **green** top on the **blue** shelf and puts the **orange** and **purple** ball in the **pink** toy box.

Noah picks up the **yellow** truck and the **brown** teddy bear. He places the **yellow** truck on the **blue** shelf and he puts the **brown** teddy bear in the **pink** toy box.

The playroom is clean!

Time for a nap!

Sweet dreams Noah and Logan.

Story Two

Noah and Logan Learn to Share

Noah and Logan are playing in the backyard.

Look, a **gray** Brontosaurus and an **orange** Stegosaurus! The dinosaurs look like fun to both Noah and Logan.

Noah picks the gray Brontosaurus and Logan picks the orange Stegosaurus. They each like playing with the dinosaur they chose.

After playing for a time, Noah decides that he would like to play with the orange Stegosaurus and Logan decides that he would like to play with the gray Brontosaurus.

"Logan," Noah says, "I would like to play with the orange Stegosaurus." "Noah," Logan says, "I would like to play with the gray Brontosaurus."

Noah and Logan have an idea! They will share the dinosaurs!

Noah gives Logan a turn to play with the gray Brontosaurus and Logan gives Noah a turn to play with the orange Stegosaurus.

Noah and Logan like sharing the dinosaurs with each other. They are both happy!

Thcy will share again tomorrow!

Story Three

Noah and Logan Learn to Tie Their Sneakers.

Foreword for parents

There are many different ways to tie sneakers and shoes. This book demonstrates the way I learned to tie my sneakers, and I still follow these steps today.

My wish is that my book will help others learn to do the same or inspire them to find their own sneaker/shoe-tying methods.

I hope you enjoy the story!

Ben Kellogg

Noah and Logan are getting ready to play outside.

They are dressed in tee shirts and shorts and have their
hats. Now, they need to put their sneakers on and tie
them!

The boys start by slipping their sneakers onto their feet.

Noah has green sneakers and Logan has red .

Noah begins tying his green sneakers. He starts by crossing the **green and black** shoelaces into an "X". Logan begins tying his sneakers in the same way.

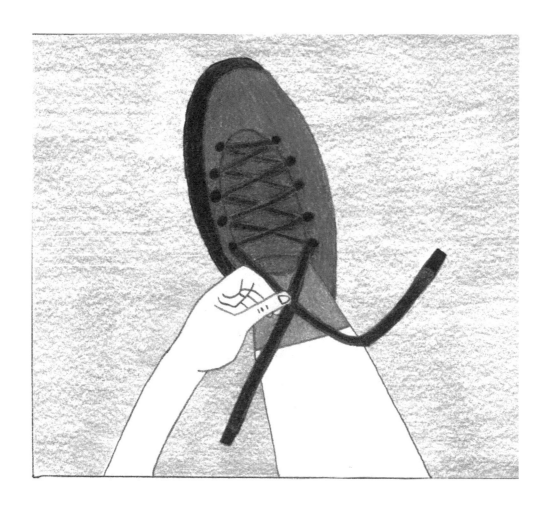

Next, Logan holds the red and black shoelaces on his red sneaker at the "X". Noah holds his shoelaces at the "X", too.

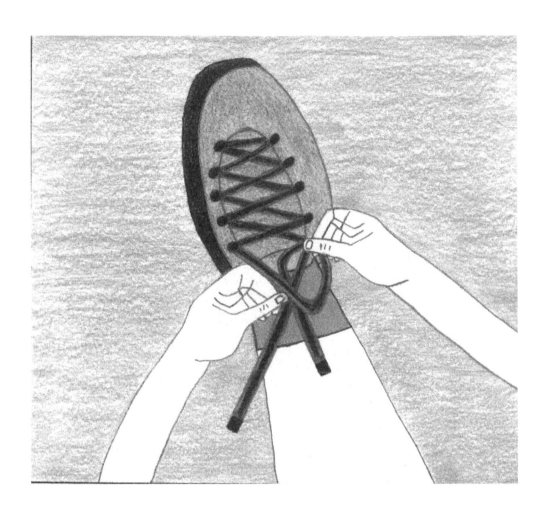

Now, Noah loops one **green and black** shoelace over
the other then pushes it around and under the "X".
Logan follows along with his shoelaces.

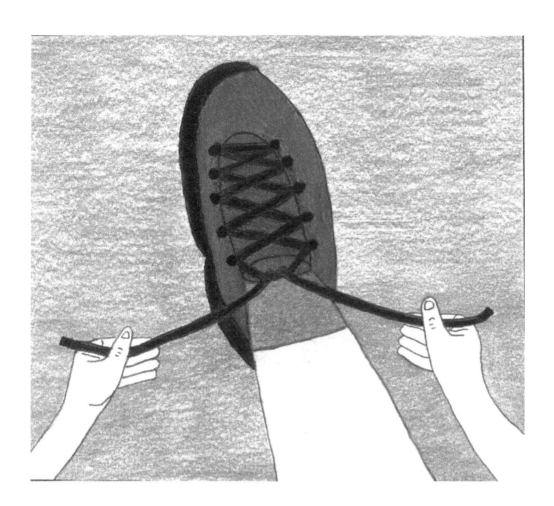

Then, Logan holds his `red and black` shoelaces at each end and pulls them into a tight knot. Noah pulls his shoelaces tight, too.

Noah then makes a loop with one **green and black** shoelace. Logan makes a loop with one of his shoelaces as well.

Next, Logan takes his other red and black shoelace
and moves it over his thumb and behind the loop. Noah
does the same thing with his shoelace.

Then, with his pointer finger, Noah pushes his **green and black** shoelace through the hole under the loop. Logan pushes his shoelace through, too.

Now, Logan pulls his red and black shoelace through the hole using his thumb and pointer finger, making another loop. Noah pulls his shoelace through and makes another loop just like Logan does.

Then, Noah holds his **green and black** shoelace loops at each end. Logan also holds his loops at each end.

Last, Logan pulls his red and black shoelace loops tightly into a bow. Noah makes a tight bow to finish tying his sneakers, too.

Hoorah!! Noah and Logan have tied their sneakers!

Noah and Logan are on their way out to play, with their sneakers on and tied! They also have their hats on and their favorite toys. Have fun Noah and Logan!

Story Four

Noah and Logan Learn to Care for Their Pets.

Noah and Logan love their pets. Noah's pet is a dog named Codi. Logan has a pet cat named Precious. They take very good care of Codi and Precious.

The boys feed their pets every day and make sure they have fresh water to drink. Logan pours cat food into Precious's bowl as Codi enjoys the dog food Noah has already poured for him. Their pets also sometimes get treats!

Noah and Logan know that exercise is important for keeping Codi and Precious healthy. Noah plays fetch with Codi who loves chasing the **yellow** ball. Precious loves to pounce on the **black** string that Logan waves for her. They play every day!

To keep their pets clean and free of fleas and ticks,
Noah and Logan give them baths. Codi and Precious
love the water!

After their baths, Precious and Codi are brushed by the boys to make their coats super shiny and soft. Brushing also helps remove their loose fur.

Noah and Logan make sure when their pets go potty
that they clean up after them. Logan cleans out
Precious's litter box whenever she uses it. Noah takes
Codi outside and cleans up after him when he is
finished going potty.

Noah and Logan take Codi and Precious for regular checkups with an animal doctor called a veterinarian to make sure they are healthy. The boys take them to the vet when they are sick, too!

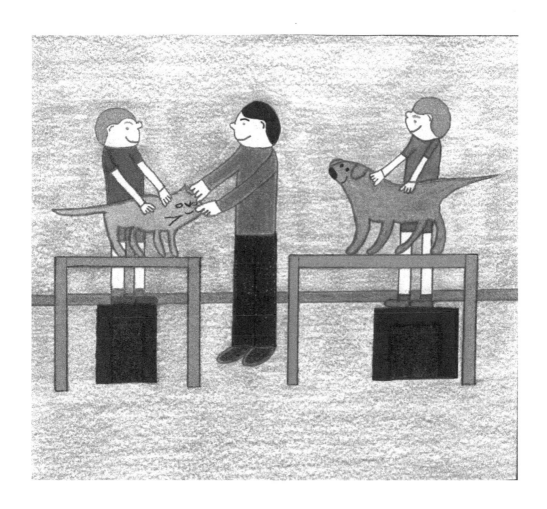

The veterinarian closely looks over both pets to make
sure they are doing well, and Precious and Codi are
given special shots to keep them from getting sick. The
vet can also give the boys' pets medicine to keep fleas
and ticks from getting on them.

By taking good care of their pets and giving them lots
of love, Noah and Logan keep Codi and Precious
healthy and happy!

Story Five

Noah and Logan Learn to Make New Friends.

Dedication: To Noah and Logan and all their cousins with love: Owen, Samantha, Leah, Ethan, Nolan, and Joshua

Noah and Logan are going to their favorite playground today. They see many other children already playing and having fun.

Noah and Logan see two boys playing on the step jungle.

They join them on the steps and Noah says, "Hi, I'm Noah and this is Logan." One of the boys says, "Hello, my name is Nolan." The other boy says, "Hi guys, I'm Joshua."

Logan asks, "Do you want to play together?" "Sure," both Nolan and Joshua answer at the same time. The new friends all play together on the step jungle.

After playing with Nolan and Joshua for a while, Noah and Logan decide they want to play on the tire swing. They say goodbye and wave to their new friends. Then they head toward the little girl on the big tire.

When the boys get to the tire swing, they introduce themselves to the little girl.

She says, "It is nice to meet you both. My name is Leah." Noah and Logan ask Leah, "Can we swing with you?" "Yes, that would be great! It is more fun playing together than playing alone," Leah says.

Noah, Logan, and Leah then take turns pushing each other on the tire swing.

Noah and Logan enjoy swinging with Leah. Then they decide to try the nearby climbing wall.

"Thanks for sharing the tire swing with us, Leah. We are going to the climbing wall now. See you later," they both say. Leah says, "Okay, I liked playing with you, too. Have fun on the wall!"

They wave goodbye to each other and Noah and Logan make their way toward the climbing wall.

As the boys get closer to the climbing wall, they see another boy at the top of the wall. "Hello up there," they call to him. "Do you want to play?" The boy answers, "Yes, that sounds like fun, come on up!"

When they reach the boy, Noah and Logan say "Hi" and tell him who they are. "Hi Noah and Logan, I'm Owen," he says, and the new friends begin to play.

Noah and Logan have a great time playing with Owen on the climbing wall.

After a time, they see two empty swings on the swing set and decide to move on to them. They tell Owen, "Climbing with you has been very fun. Thanks for playing with us; we think we will try the swing set now. It was nice meeting you!" "I had fun too! Enjoy the swings, guys," Owen answers.

The boys climb down and wave goodbye to Owen.

Noah and Logan say "Hello," climb onto the swings, and tell the two children already swinging on the swing set their names.

The little girl says, "Hello, I'm Samantha." The little boy says, "Hi, my name is Ethan." "It is nice to meet you both," Noah and Logan answer. "Great to meet you, too," their new friends reply.

They all have fun on the swing set.

After all four children tire of swinging on the swing set, Noah and Logan ask Samantha and Ethan if they would like to meet all their other new friends. Samantha and Ethan say, "Yes, we would love to meet everyone!"

Noah and Logan call to each of their new friends and ask, "Would you like to play together on the step jungle?" Everyone agrees and they all meet at the step jungle.

All the children say "Hello" to each other, introduce themselves, and play on the step jungle together. They all have a fantastic time!

Soon it is time for Noah and Logan to go home. All of their new friends say "Goodbye" and wave to the boys.

Noah and Logan cannot wait to see them again!

And Now

Both the author Benjamin Kellogg and Ex-L-Ence Publishing hope that you have enjoyed reading these stories.

Please tell people about this Book, write a review or mention it on your favourite social networking site.

For further titles that may be of interest to you as well as forthcoming books by Benjamin, please visit the Ex-L-Ence website at www.ex-l-ence.com where you can optionally join an information list.

CPSIA information can be obtained
at www.ICGtesting.com
Printed in the USA
FSHW04n1349150318
45488FS